DOGS WHO SMILE

EBURY
PRESS

1 3 5 7 9 10 8 6 4 2

First published in 2012 by Ebury Press, an imprint of Ebury Publishing
A Random House Group company

The Random House Group Limited Reg. No. 954009

Addresses for companies within the Random House Group can be found at
www.randomhouse.co.uk

A CIP catalogue record for this book is available from the British Library

The Random House Group Limited supports The Forest Stewardship Council®(FSC®), the leading
international forest certification organisation. Our books carrying the FSC label are printed on
FSC® certified paper. FSC is the only forest certification scheme endorsed by the leading
environmental organisations, including Greenpeace. Our paper procurement policy can be found at
www.randomhouse.co.uk/environment

Printed and bound in China by Toppan Leefung

ISBN 9780091947255

To buy books by your favourite authors and register for offers visit
www.randomhouse.co.uk

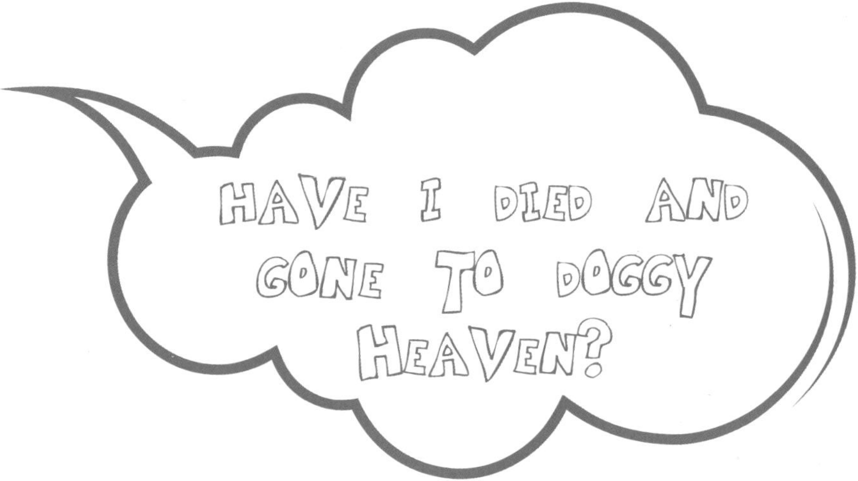
HAVE I DIED AND GONE TO DOGGY HEAVEN?

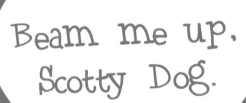

"And don't even think about blaming that one on me..."

Hey! Who turned the lights out?

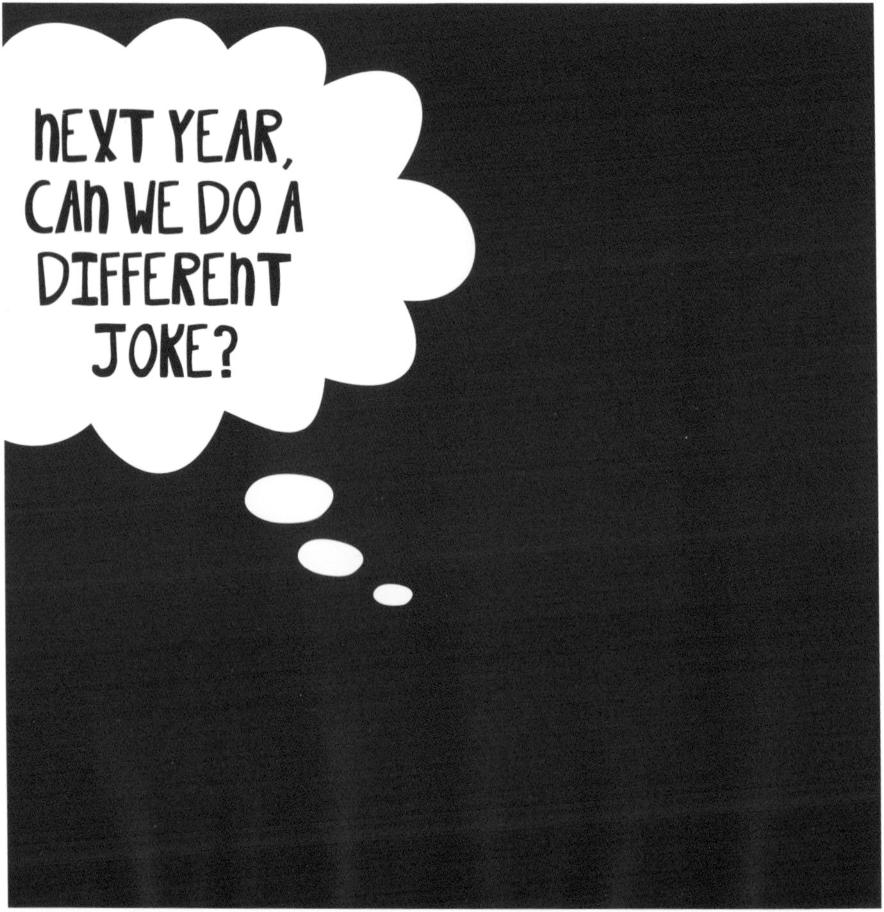
NEXT YEAR, CAN WE DO A DIFFERENT JOKE?

"Quick! Dude! YouTube this!"

"OK, SO FIRST WE HIT THE CLEAN SHEETS, THEN ROLL ON THE WHITE CARPET..."

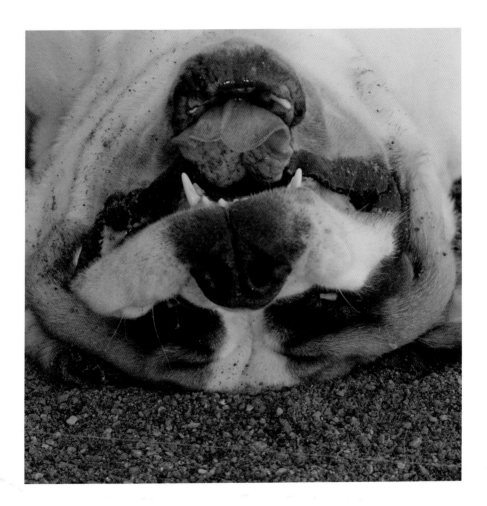

"GIMME FIIIIIVE!"

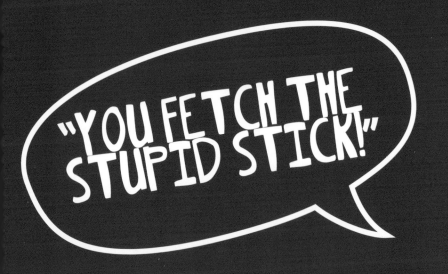

This hair clip's too tight... I can't close my eyes!

HAVE YOU NEVER HEARD OF A DOG NAP?

"You sit and throw, I run and fetch. It's a win-win situation!"

"ALL TOGETHER NOW... DOGGY PADDLE!"

"come on, give us a kiss!"

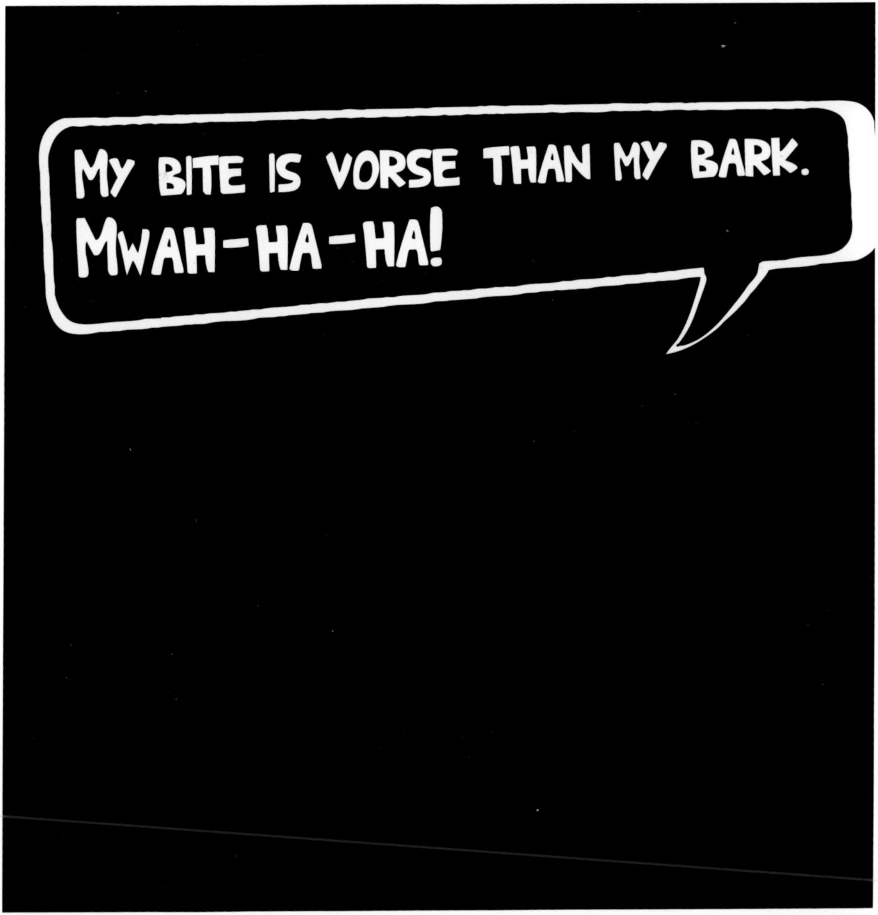
MY BITE IS VORSE THAN MY BARK. MWAH-HA-HA!

WELL SOMEBODY'S GOTTA USE MUM'S FITNESS DVD...

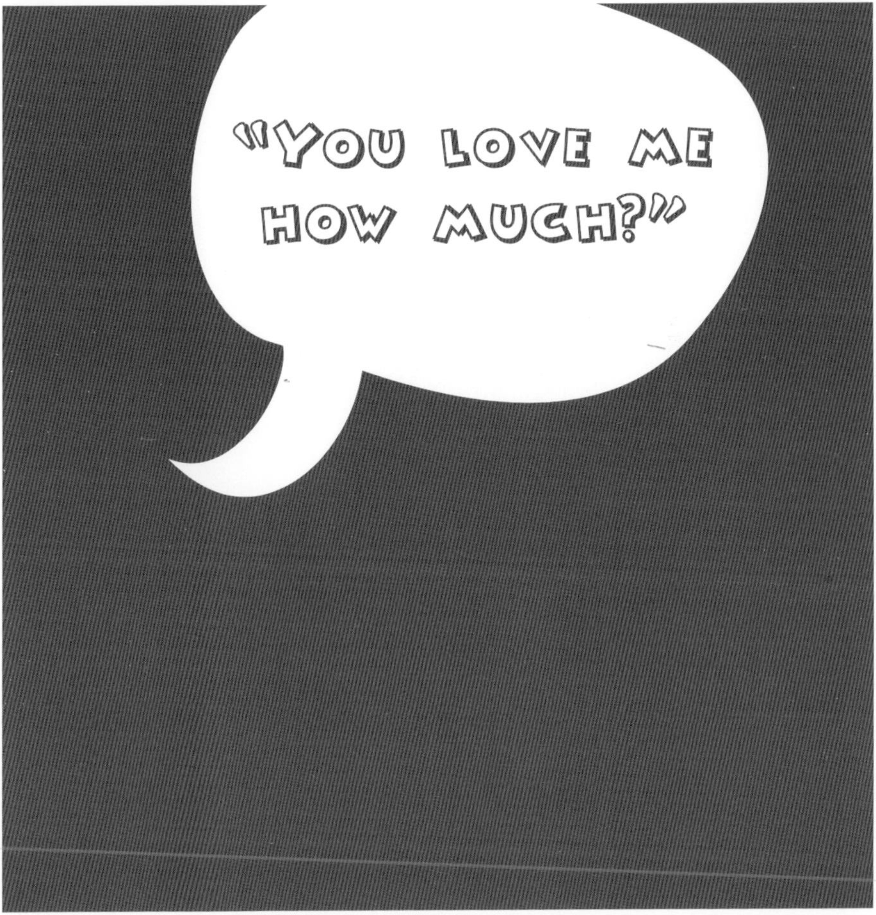
"YOU LOVE ME HOW MUCH?"

"IF I SQUINT, THE POSTMAN WILL THINK I'M SLEEPING, AND THEN... BANG!"

HI, MY NAME IS MAX. AND MY SPECIALIST SUBJECT IS LAMPPOSTS OF THE WORLD

"See this arrow?
Apply biscuits
now!"

JUST SMILE AND IT'LL
SOON BE OVER...

"MAYBE THE WIND MACHINE WAS A BAD IDEA?"

"BE HONEST, DOES THIS COLLAR MAKE MY EARS LOOK BIG?"

"UP A BIT,
LEFT A
BIT... THAT'S
NIIIIICE!"

WHO. ARE. YOU. CALLING. A. SAUSAGE?!

I know she's
starting to look
like me... It kinda
creeps me out...

Picture Credits